Spiritual Chiaroscuro

BRIAN ALTHOFF

NEWMAN SPRINGS PUBLISHING
320 Broad Street
Red Bank, NJ 07701

First originally published by Newman Springs Publishing 2024

ISBN 979-8-89061-320-2 (Paperback)
ISBN 979-8-89061-321-9 (Digital)

Printed in the United States of America

To my beloved Bosco, see you in time.

Different Landscapes

I have seen perfect framed landscapes
In which the genius of some artist adds that light,
That spark to get under the surface of what is there.
I have felt the peace and escape for which I have longed.
Yet, in reality, nature falls flat.
Reality leaves much to be desired.
That is the difference in what is framed
And what is before one's own eyes.

Never Surprised

It is a world in which the majority choose a convenient blindness
While everything hints too much of too little
And the air is scented with a violent tension.
No imagination could conjure up anything as lurid and horrible.
Reality leaves no surprises.
Anything is possible, and the worst is expected.
The definition of humanity is hopelessly vague and flawed,
As life is painful contradictions and unsettling histories.

An Endless Repeating

There is a void in life that cannot be denied,
Every minute of every day, over and over again.
It is the same life repeating itself with boredom as its ruler.
All actions become repeated,
All emotions once lived become less visceral with time.
Nothing is new, nothing remains to be seen.
It is the repetition which drives me to a certain madness.
It is the expectation of absolutely nothing which causes
    inexpressible despair.
There is a paralysis which hits the mind every morning,
When awakened from sleep into an uncontrollable awareness
    of nothing.

Osmosis

Many moments are spent wrapped in irritability and depression
When emotion has floored me and the words are evasive.
Just the act of daily living is unbearable.
I wait for the words, I wait, and I wait
Yet there is no worthwhile osmosis,
No way to transfer onto paper
The emotion without the words.

A War That Is Never Won

My greatest conflict has been with myself a war within
Where I play victim, judge, and executioner.
It is an endless dualism
Where self-pity meets self-loathing.
I heap great amounts of doubt upon myself always.
One minute I am sure of myself,
The next minute I break everything apart.
I have never allowed myself any emotional safe haven.
It is as if I would not feel complete
Unless I was at odds with something always.
It is a war that is never won.
It is a life that will not allow me to live.

Everpresent, Everywhere

There is a tragedy so deep and profound within life
That it is usually beyond notice or understanding.
It exists within the lurid media stories,
In the workplace, in the home, and in the mind,
Although it is never truly defined.
It exists in the morning, in the afternoon, and in the dark of night
It comes alive in our many disappointments,
In our dying hospital beds and in our various quarrels.
It flashes its true colors in the eyes of the resigned and beaten.
It mocks the doctors in the institutions and asylums.
It taunts those jailed in prisons
As it destroys the humanity of those jailed.
It makes our existence become that question
Repeated over and over again throughout time:
The question of why.
It is the element of that tragedy which makes us forget the why.
It weakens our imaginations
Until we settle for the mundane and the small pleasantries
Which in reality are all we have,
And that is the true tragedy.

Very Few Heroes

There are very few who have ever lived
Who would die for truth.
In fact, fewer know how to even be true to themselves.
Truth is ironically obvious.
It is an overwhelming factor undeniable in existence.
Each closing day brings with it the truth,
The truth of life discarded for cheap tokens
Gained while realizing with painful nostalgia
How hard it is to live for yourself
In a world which prefers lies.

Possession

It is only when words fail me
That I realize I have felt something profound.
Those brief moments when the hair rises on the back of my neck
And my insides are hollow,
My mind and soul understand something in unison,
Something beyond tragedy,
Which nothing can perfectly describe.
It is as if all those shadows that converge upon my mind,
The ghosts that materialize just from living,
Emerge into the light and become this emotional insight
That strikes like lighting before retiring back into the dark.
I am awed to feel something which hits like that,
And at once this indescribable emotion makes all of life
A feeling tears could not express.

5:30 p.m. on a Thursday

Everything at first is an open door
Which in our curiosity can be great,
Until we walk through the wrong door
Which shuts behind our youth,
Trapping and altering the course of our lives.

Always Running Away

The memories will always remain,
All those awkward moments of which
I wanted no part.
Inside I either trembled with fear or rage,
Wanting and hoping for a quick exit,
Maybe even a sprinkling of invisible dust,
Anything but having to face conflict.
I know the reality of cowardice and all its ramifications,
For my selfish nature wants an inner peace,
Wants to hear only my voice and not the voice of someone else.
Call me what I expect to hear: an asshole, a coward,
A man refusing to face a reality which differs from what he wants.
I define those weak traits,
But then for whom do I live?

Escaping Winter

Flying towards their destination
Free in perfect flight are the birds
Against the backdrop of winter's approaching sky.
Here I stand grounded, grounded
To this concrete where I can only look above
And dream of flight
It all seems so dull,
These short yet long days of nothings,
No backdrop for me to silhouette across,
No destination, no tangible dream.
I am living life by calendar days, by clocks
Nowhere close to actual moments
Where life is lived,
Instead blindly automatic, piloting
With no direction, no grace.
Grandiose thoughts fill me up,
Only to deflate come nightfall
When everything I just lived
Will once again repeat in a few hours.
Sleep is the elixir in this present time,
Sleep which knows no gravity, no demands.
Only in sleep do I forget this weight, this mind
The birds fly past leaving no trace of their existence,
A brief moment of nature's artistry,
And a bitter reminder that I stand motionless.

Introspection

I am always one thought past the awareness of the moment,
Like someone talking yet miles away from the conversation,
Or suddenly realizing the awareness of the time
And how I had become lost in a busy house.
These thoughts carry me away,
These distractions take me away from myself and isolate me.
It is not that I am unable to appreciate
The peaceful, fleeting moments which occur,
But it is as if I am never truly grounded in myself.
It is a feeling of pressure, anxiety and a sadistic streak
To be masochistic to myself:
An unending introspection that never allows peace.
I can never truly relax within those moments
Where one is afforded that brief luxury.
I have a burning desire to be released.
But the reality is like one of an aimless cloud
Disappearing into the sky.
More and more I am drifting into myself:
Always to know the burden of my being.

To Try and Hold On

I have never doubted miracles.
Once in a great while man can find a loophole
To believe in something.
It is certain though that doubt can blister the brain,
And the tests, the negativity can run rampant
Throughout the days, months, and years.
After years of expecting more and receiving less
The idea of a miracle seems less certain.
Life disappears from the eyes, life becomes less of a gift,
And days become less of a celebration and more like endless work.
But deep within I still want to believe.
I still want my childhood dreams and belief back.
I do not want to relinquish that small thread of hope
Which keeps me from falling into a complete living death.
The words uttered "hold on" can do wonders,
But I can only wonder for how long
Before everything sinks into itself and is lost.

Malignant

The state of the heart is always a precarious one.
Everything is fragile, and nothing in life retains an image
That would give hope of an impenetrable beauty
Which would always shine.
The heart's trust starts as a priceless gift,
Then it becomes something of a laugh.
See how quickly innocence is erased from a child's vision,
Only to be replaced with hardened cynicism.
The heart allows lovers a short taste of sweet bliss,
But quickly reveals the center of this union
As hollow and void of substance.
People have followed their heart
And run off the octane of their dreams,
Only to crash and burn into the wall
Of an apathetic, indifferent reality.
Many evenings the heart along with the mind
Has soaked in liquor or wallowed in drugs
To try to rid it of the growing malignancy
Festering within, eating at us.
We weep for our lost humanity
While we crush and destroy that of someone else.
The heart's bitterness has created a climate that never changes.
It is here for every new life born.
It is only a matter of time
Until everyone experiences the reality of pain.

A War That Is Never Won

My greatest conflict has been with myself: a war within
Where I play victim, judge and executioner.
It is an endless dualism
Where self-pity meets self-loathing.
I heap great amounts of doubt upon myself always.
One minute I am sure of myself,
The next minute I break everything apart.
I have never allowed myself any emotional safe haven.
It is as if I would not feel complete
Unless I was at odds with something always.
It is a war that is never won.
It is a life that will not allow me to live.

Talking Loud and Doing Nothing

Away from the situation, away from certain ears
In the safety of my home and with a few drinks in me
I am transformed into the bold tough commentator
Demanding attention and respect for my numerous grievances
While sitting on my drunken throne watching those here listening
To see if my points have been drilled into their minds.
Nothing is spared my sarcasm.
I only get louder and louder, especially if challenged.
The last commentary was spoken
Nearing the end of an unusually hellish workweek.
My God, the venom I mustered up was incredible.
I ranted and raved on those at my house that night
You should have seen my courage at work the next morning,
Greeting the boss and answering his dull, trite questions
With the respect of a subordinate slave.

Smile within a Mist

Such a gentle, warm smile,
Such grace spreading goodwill upon a moment.
The smile has no face, no eyes, no definite features,
But I see this image in calm moments,
Moments where I can reflect
Upon that which could be comforting.
I see a body, coquettish
And beautiful with open arms
And no notion of leaving my side.
I see other bodies and faces,
But none offer this form of love.
Imagination creates this dilemma,
But who knows?
One day that smile might match a face
And match a soul with an undying desire
To know love inside and out.

Memories Becoming Clearer

The task of an autobiography
Is almost too much.
The pain of remembering
What once was buried,
And the realization of how petty
My life looks on paper,
Brings the knowledge of being
A complete, utter fool.
But knowledge comes from experience,
And a weight is being taken off my shoulders.
Baptism comes from total self-introspection.
Moving on requires unlocking dusty skeletons
And throwing away the key which hides them,
The key of modesty and fear.
To bury embarrassment is to never get over it.
To bury stupidity is to never get wiser.
To bury my life is to kill it.

Scapegoats for Our Frustrations

A sweeping frustration mounts gaining stupendous momentum,
An ignorant frustration attacks the mind and soul.
Through enraged blindness we look for a scapegoat.
Legal bloodletting in any way
Gives an excitement that could only come
From the depths of hell itself.
Men use morals as an excuse.
How will blood redeem that which is gone forever?
Death should not be ordained
Upon anybody with false moral righteousness.
Our mistakes only too clearly shine
Upon those who serve as examples for us,
But we fail to see that.
We are too scared to do the job ourselves.
We have paid murderers killing for us
Who hide behind the government.
We are all guilty of spilt blood.
We are all guilty of false morals.
We are all guilty of hypocrisy.
We are an impotent nation
Unable to clearly see where we are heading,
Unable to clearly rationalize our deeds.
We heap collective guilt
Then go on a killing spree.

Cheers

Along with the tears,
Comes false sentimentality.
One too many beers,
and now you appear
Somewhat thoughtful about your past.
What problem was there before?
It seems you had none,
Brushing things off
And letting bad blood buildup.
You see no correlation
Between your sorrow
And maybe the sorrow you caused.
Add things up, well what now?
As soon as the drunk wears off:
Will you still be reflective and
Wanting to pay penance?
It is too bad having to be
Under a guise to be real,
Or to be reflective.
The mind under the double-edged sword
Of substance, either quiet and stoic,
Or malicious or teary-eyed or comic.
It is hard to see into one's reality
When they are never consistent,
When they are always avoiding the eyes,
When they are weekend drunks
And become sloppy and lack integrity.
Salud! And cheers to regret.

Learning to Stand By Yourself

The sadness of change,
The shifting of personality,
The shut door of friendship,
Being left in the cold
With your old traditions,
With your unyielding integrity,
With your anger.
The ungraspable reasons
To bang your fist against a wall
Because you notice things disintegrating
Before your very eyes,
Wanting the clearness of vision,
Wishing those around you could see
Where they're taking themselves.
Call it stupidity
Call it drugs,
Call it women,
Call it disinterest,
Call it work,
Call it money,
Call it anything,
It all chalks up to change.
Things will never be the same.

Abrasion

Why is it so easy to inadvertently hurt someone who came
    with goodwill
But at a time when the last thing you wanted was help or company?
You shot off an abrasive comment leaving one hurt and confused.
The guilt comes later with the question of your own decency.
Apologies become complicated with emotional fatigue and regret.
But the words were born of your mind and came out of
    your mouth.
It's too easy to be complicated, opinionated, hard to be around.
Without realizing it, you alienate yourself
Or disguise your hate to avoid an even bigger problem.

Youth

Oh, the recklessness that resides in all of us
The stupidity that kills us or our fellow man.
Irresponsibility seems as linked to us as our DNA.
To be young and foolish is natural,
To be young and restless is natural,
But any human being can do brash, foolish stunts.
It's only when you can vindicate your behavior
That just maybe you're not an idiot, but lost,
And we're all lost.

Smoke

I let out a gigantic cloud of smoke
Which lingers in the air, stagnant and cancerous.
I imagine that within that cloud are my problems,
Worries exhaled leaving me
Breathless, absolved, and relaxed.
Instead I choke on the realization
That there is no wishing away or eliminating
The smoke of ruin and discontent
Which lays trapped within my chest,
Building up blackness,
Cancerous and full of premature death.

Something Real

I think of others having content evenings,
Quiet dinners, quiet minds, quiet lives.
Sometimes that state is envious.
Where did the quiet road pass me?
Where can I revert back to a calm collective?
The paths I trod are strewn with broken glass and screaming,
Yet there will be no new behavior modification.
I need something real,
Some mental or physical stimulation.
Guesses from short lived experiences lead me to think
That the only way for me to be docile
Will be for my neck to get snapped
Or from a frontal lobotomy,
And that scares the shit out of me.
Uncontrollable emotions and actions
Leading only to sorrow and destruction
To only understand the one thing
Which I've completely understood.
Fear.

Life's Long, Silly Games

Human emotions and human behaviors range from pathetic
To ridiculous, to outright mysterious.
It seems as if the need for praise and attention
Drives even the most independent of us all
It is always proven over and over.
Watch gatherings from school dances to church on Sundays,
Watch the busy sidewalks, the packed malls, and grocery stores.
Watch the swaggers, the grimaces, and the body language
Exhibited for show.
See how a taste of power or a change of uniform
Makes a change of person.
Listen to the conversations that always give away
The shallowness and the hint of bravado people carry.
It is a conditioning of the masses
That allows us to accept intolerable egos.
Everything about people becomes some game,
Some performance, some role.
Everything real becomes buried, and although known,
It becomes less important than the social show.
All this for praise, for attention,
For a pleasurable masturbation of the ego.
It is as if we stay children always, only the older we get,
The more silly and pseudo-complicated we become
With the power to make others obey,
Which is beyond frightening.
It is as if people forget the existence of mortality,
And that it is neither sensible nor good to waste what little
    they have
All over these pathetic, lifelong games.

If Everything Could Stay New

Staring at foreign walls
In a foreign room
Within a foreign city,
Mind blank, pure calm
While outside the city moves,
The dark falls,
Alone with your worries,
People's indifference is like heaven.
Your only concern is yourself.
As soon as things become familiar
Everything turns sour again.
You're now a familiar face
Assimilated into the scene.
To belong you need a job,
Money and all the other commodities.
That's when restlessness sinks in,
When life becomes dull and predictable,
But to be a foreigner, to never settle
Is to know moments of calm
Which is almost a paradox,
A calm within a restless moving.

To Hold Just a Little Back

Sometimes a healthy dose of surprise helps human survival.
When you let known your true self
You give all of yourself away for the taking.
For some reason we like the mystery,
We like figuring out an entire person,
Then often discard him as quick as we found him.
But when you hold back, you hold some element of mystery,
A backdrop at your disposal to keep someone on his toes,
A way to keep some of yourself intact.
To be somewhat secretive can save you pain.
We like so much to flay each other alive.
To keep mistrust rampant.
After a while we learn how to lucratively lie,
All for power and a false sense of security.
Can we really honestly relate to one another
And build a beautiful bond with two independent souls?
Can we really shed skeletons in our dusty closets
To let known our most inner fears and desires?
I would like to think so,
But scattered success stories don't restore
My faith in the human soul.
Our self-esteem is as fragile as glass.
It wilts as easy as flowers.
Our mentality is one in dire need of acceptance.
We find means to fill our gigantic need for love,
We fill our black void with perversions
Doing so with desperate spontaneity.

We do a lot without much thought, but my God
What won't we do to escape confusion and pain?
Longing is the most horrendous ordeal.
In your mind it's crystal clear what you want.
Unfortunately on the opposite end, the feeling is not the same.
We need to find some morality for our disarrayed lives,
We need to start doing things seriously and thoroughly.

The China Doll Syndrome

Let me take you off your mantle,
You're so dusty, so dusty you look dead.
Your alabaster face is smudged with dirt.
Too many people have touched and soiled you,
You poor, poor doll.
Your eyes don't retain the life they used to.
I have to be careful not to break you;
You're so fragile my poor china doll.
Be animate, be in my world!
What would I do if you cracked into little bits:
Fine dust to be blown away.
I'm so pathetic wishing that my head overloads
Porcelain dust in my eyes and mouth,
The bitter taste of reality,
The dust of disassembled beauty.

Man on a Couch

Sitting in a darkened apartment
Midafternoon noises from the street outside
Remind you that something is going on
While you sit watching cheap soap operas.
Midthirties, unemployed and uninterested,
Quite content to do nothing, yet upset
With your finances, children, and neighborhood.
Eating cheap potato chips while sipping on a 40 oz.
Mind in neutral, hand-to-mouth action.
You watch the commercials for new cars, clothes, restaurants,
No entertainment for a man with 65 cents in his pocket
And a freezer full of cheap dinners, lunchmeat, and beer.
You see the commercials for trade schools but those cost money,
And they want the young, naive recruits,
Not some middle-aged, cynical, impoverished man
With years stacked upon worthless years.
Your only entertainment is getting drunk and maybe
Banging some low-class, dumpy bitch you met in the neighborhood bar.
Life can be totally meaningless.
One fucked up year of your life can change you forever,
Can ruin you, pick up your whimsy body
And put you in places you never dreamed of.
Some of your friends don't work either
But with disabilities and that hardened look
A forty-hour, menial labor week gives a human face,
They find that they keep striking out.
There are those so ignorant, so naive, so inhuman
That they preach abolishment of government funds like welfare,
Stating that those on it can work if they want to.
Yet they won't hire them or give them a second glance,
Those nameless faces each deserving what isn't given to them:
A fucking chance.

Death Comes in Many Forms

Let me kiss your bony knuckles, Death.
You come in one smooth package wrapped up in glamor and fame.
We use your slow suicide toys: liquor, sex, cigarettes, hedonism,
    and sadism.
You are in all our minds once the animal instinct is loose.
The body with its weaknesses feeds off the instinct for pleasure
While death talks sweetly to the animal in you,
And it always seems to make sense and sound like fun.
The suffering drown in your tides of escape, your smooth ways
    of easy death.
In shapes of bullets and steel the lost pop you into a chamber
And you do the rest of the work.
Fearless and formless, you lurk all around.
No one can stop you, the Inevitable End.
No one really thinks of the extreme totality of death.

Up in Flames

We get comfort in constantly keeping
People around our orbit.
It does not matter
How we really feel about them.
All that matters
Is if these people need us.
We like abandon: it feels nice
To avoid morals and good taste.
We have the fortitude of a maggot.
We claim love,
While we ceremoniously destroy
Truth and trust.
All this in the name of amusement.
There is an innate cruelty in us
That destroys the beauty also in us.
Our beauty is a well-kept secret.
Introverted and hard to find.
If we do not get too wrapped
In cruelty,
Maybe we can find and foster
Our souls, our true beauty.
Why do we waste our lives
In pursuit of dragging everything
Down in shit?

Nothing has meaning or value,
Unless we want to place
Meaning or value to it.
It is so goddamn hard
For people to interact.
One person is only along
For the ride,
While the other person wants
To build a foundation.
The whole fucking mess
Goes up in flames.

Keeping That Ideal

Purveying the high life,
With an envy of abandon,
A desire for escape,
A knowing of coming to an end,
Totally crashing down upon everything
With a violent fury,
Endurance and patience
Can sometimes leave you,
But there is a simple logic involved,
And no matter how lost you get,
That logic never leaves you.
That logic is of abandon,
Of death,
Of knowing your limits,
Of knowing your mortality,
Of knowing your weaknesses,
Of knowing fundamental truths.
When things come full circle,
Come hell or high water,
Where are the golden palaces,
Do they even exist?
Is this just a game where all lose?
Full circle, where will you end?
Will you realize that you have kept your integrity
And won,
Or will you realize only the wicked gain?
You can easily forget
All the trivial aspects and thoughts
Upon your life.
Keep that one ideal
That keeps you going
No matter how simple

No matter how destructive.
Your integrity is your heart and soul.
Never abandon that which is honest.
High life is total living,
Is never copping out because of someone else
Or because of material gain.
High life is knocking life on its ass,
Then smirking while growing in spirit.
How can you grow
When you just accept blindly?
Mistakes cause prosperity
If you realize them.
Fuck boredom,
Fuck all standards,
Fuck everything that does not make you grow.
As long as you respect yourself,
Who do you have to answer to?
Just be decent enough
To own up to your life
And your mistakes.
Obtain your goals
And define the existence you created.
Abandon is losing yourself among truth,
Giving yourself over to your ideals.
You speak your mind
And get regarded with laughs,
You get blackballed,
But to go on is abandon,
Is living the high life.

Retirement

When you're no longer worth anything in the workforce,
When you're tired and old,
When things don't come as fast as they used to,
Get ready to become a burden,
Feeling like a weight on your children's back,
Feeling less than human
When your body won't behave like it used to.
So many placid faces at rest homes
Propped up cute and senile for death,
Put in a place to sit, be quiet, be forgotten.
Imagine sitting and looking out a window,
But not being able to go out and live,
Or have a wealth of happiness come over you
Just because you get a visit, a guilt-ridden visit.
We live in the kind of country where you'd better hope
When old age hits, you still cope like a younger person
Because most people have no respect for their elders.

No Connection Here

People talk of love
Like it is a high and lofty word,
But there are forms of love
For one's physical well-being
And one's mental and spiritual well-being.
Too many people feel misunderstood
And that feeling is one of isolation and dejection.
No matter how much skin warmth you have around you
A link is missing and arguments and hatred arise.
Too much meaning and emphasis is placed
On something that is either there or it is not.
It is a gift that comes through luck,
Not the statistics of relationships.
Who cannot find somebody?
But is there that special someone?
Most people place ignorance in their minds
When devoting themselves to someone.
It makes shit comfortable.
It kills the clarity of maybe seeing
A mistake taking place.
When you can comfort someone mentally,
That is the best gift and form of love.
It is a bond between two unique people
That can overcome differences
And lift the soul to a higher ground.
We can die in vain searching
For that special someone.
But at least we are not selling ourselves out
To the first available piece of ass,
Or to the first person who would tell us
What we want to hear before turning on us.

What Can You Do?

Control:
The clipping of a young bird's wings,
Then putting a sheet over the cage
When it finally starts to sing.
Control:
That which destroys trust,
That mimics only hatred
And ignorance.
Control:
Assumption of the many guises
Of love, religion, work.
Control:
Your own mind
The worst prison
Which has total control.
It will only feed you more
Misconstrued meanings of life.
There is no escape
From the sentence of control.
Your steps are watched
With total scrutiny.
You are the world's piece
Of breathing clay
To mold and squeeze,
To mold and squeeze,
To squeeze and suffocate.

To Spit Only Bile

I wake up to what is left of the still remnants of my mind,
I have that sour, bitter taste of another morning
Of remembering another night, words forgotten,
Those problems before still bothersome, lifeless fruitful.
I will always replace worries with a new set of worries,
I will always replace problems with a new set of problems
I will always lick my lips like a hungry wolf
With the knowledge of getting myself into a deeper pit.
I am so goddamned thirsty and tired
Tired of all these eye sores
Tired of all this fucking waste
This sickness that builds up and leaves one's eyes blank and dull
To need a "human" savior
A Christ with a cup of wine
A Christ with love and forgiveness and understanding
A Christ with flaws and eternal redemption
But all I have are my own two broken wings.

Our Playful Spirits

We understand and crave that sweet taste of sin
We love our dirty little secrets
That feeling of electricity.
That feeling of blasphemy,
That feeling of pounding blood in the temples
Of our engulfed minds preoccupied by temptation,
By the beauty of the casual moment,
By the insanity of action and reaction.
Our spontaneous ways will get the best of us.
Morality is a word for the weak.
The sins we do, the dramas we dream,
The things we deny, the horrors we become,
The playboy, the shrewd bitch, the calculating criminal.
No one wants to own up to the pile of shit,
The tears they have created,
But the tax collector comes
And sometimes the fee cannot be paid.

Totally Spent

Sadly spent sentiment,
One only too glad to revel in the warmth
While another shivered from nonreciprocal feelings
Of an unbalanced love.
One felt, the other didn't, at least not the same.
The injustice, the nicks in the heart,
Every second consumed with a fire
Only one could extinguish.
After a while there was not even kind sentiment,
Only a few words, a passing glance, a cold stare.

Why Do I Do This to Myself?

The pain of loving another person
Who is only using me
As a stepping stone for her wants
Is almost too much.
I do not want to acknowledge
The fact that I love in vain,
That my passion is only fuel
To the consuming fire.
As long as I continue to love
I am a shoulder to cry upon,
An ear to talk into,
An extra backbone for support,
Or a warm body to love
If the bottom of the barrel
Needs to be scraped.
Yet if I am honest,
I will probably receive a dishonest answer.
I will hear what I want to hear,
And I will have a warm body
Pressed against mine,
And while trying to get angry,
I will soften and release that anger.
I will buy into another lie.
It gets to the point of sheer insanity
Choking back tears while trying
To salvage what little pride I have.
Love plays no universal theme,
For what I perceive to be reality
Is only another person's fantasy game,
Another's waste of time.

Sometimes it is best not to have loved
No matter what the old theme
On the subject says,
For the pain of knowing
That I am not good enough
Is never worth falling in love
It is better to be lonely than to love
Under nonreciprocal circumstances
And still sleep alone.
This love I have is a fiery love,
One that eats me up,
One that keeps me hinged
To something that will never be,
One that will not be extinguished,
Because I have no one to put out the fire.

The Head

With nothing to stare at except the head of one in front of me
I am struck by its unusualness:
The oily secretions and strands of off-color hair.
Still, except for occasional movements and low-key murmurs.
Holding thoughts inside, this head
Can feel pain, love, kill, and create.
I sit transfixed looking at this balding scalp;
I wonder why I am even focused on this head,
Not knowing the owner of this all too human body.
It is disturbing, this still reality of flesh and blood,
This disgusting simplicity of a complex animal.

Sideline Commentator

It is interesting listening
To the people who stand on the sidelines
Complain or give lofty ideas about life
And the actions that spring from it.
They release such rancor,
And they talk such trash
That one would figure
They either had done it
Or been there.
But it is quite the opposite.
It is like all those fanatical sports fans
Who give advice to the television
Throughout a game.
If they were ex-players
Or even playing, then maybe
They would have the right
To run their mouths.
If we have not done something
We have not the right
To complain or get moral.
Laws in general were composed
On a sideline perspective,
Written out of the fear
That security would be disrupted.
It is our fear of failure
Which makes us mediocre.
It is our fear which prods us
To judge and be self-righteous.

Most people do not even realize
How boring and judgmental they are.
How to lie and save face
Has been taught us since day one.
It is the sorrow of perfection,
It is the sickness of coming in first place.
Who does not want that?
But we are not untouchable
And when we stand about
With others and gossip,
We are less than the person
Who is being talked about.
We will come off like we know
Every fucking thing in the world.
But half the time we have never been
In another's shoes.

The Pain of Remembering What Was

What did the pretense of our conversations mean?
The words were there,
Now I see they lacked feeling.
What is intellect without soul?
What is the point of talking
If your talk is cheap?
Our friendship was only a prologue
To an exciting novel never started.
Goals, my friend, what do they amount to?
Are they easily replaced and forgotten?
The stupor I live in has been disorienting
Because two connectors forming a solid chain
Has disjoined and unraveled.
Our universes are forever separated.
The logic in this is that this is life.
Small explainable differences
Turned you into putty.
Dependency is a weakness
I am finding out.
Was the pain of hell too great for you?
Do not put people in a mental museum
And outdate them,
Only to dig them out when lonely.
It is not fair to both parties.

Level of Pretentiousness

The level of pretentiousness in art runs rampant.
It all has to deal with the pain and the point of creation.
Artists feel driven to portray feelings or social commentary,
A message of some sort.
But too many artists try to be overtly intellectual,
Or overtly pointless,
And they cannot explain what they do and why.
Too many artists think that they are insightful
Because everything really is point of view.
But if one has integrity and a shred of creativity,
Then one should think before trying to produce art,
Because there is nothing worse than a pretentious, intellectual artist
Who is nothing, who understands nothing, who produces nothing.

Simple Breathing

Listening to your breathing all is simple.
Nothing remains but a soft sound
In the dark with no eyes open
No sentence emitted from the mouth.
It is better this way.
Stay asleep, stay simple,
Stay pure and angelic.
God only knows what tomorrow will bring
To your wicked mind.
Tomorrow is a dull light,
The sun means nothing but busy, hectic sounds.
These walls know more truth
Than anyone could even imagine.
They feel those haunted eyes questioning,
Just staring aimlessly
At the white paint turning yellowish and old.
When your small private space holds you captive
To taunt and derange your mind,
It will either make you stronger or destroy you.
These walls hold knowledge
And hear every quiet, disturbing thought.
It is your knowledge they know,
The only knowledge which counts.
Get to the barren level of not expecting anything,
Get to the level of one day being your own happiness.
These thoughts pass out of me
While listening to your shallow breathing.
Simple makes sense, the simpler the truer.

Alone

Going to bed alone is boring.
All you hear in your head are cars going by.
All you see are lights reflecting on your wall,
Then disappearing, all dark again.
Voices bounce off your brain
Echoing the evening and your actions
And your mind is racing.
Conversations with yourself get too one-sided.
How about some silk skin sliding upon you,
Some hands smoothing out the aches in your neck,
Laying on your back staring up at a smile
Instead of a dark ceiling.
Savor the flavor of love,
Feeling warm lips all over and the act of the quiet evening
Of which you can only dream.
This evening the sheets will be cold,
The mind will taunt, race, and land in a foreign gutter
Somewhere in the far reaches of Neverland.
Tossing and turning won't do a damn bit of good
For the human nightmare, loneliness.

A Series of Unanswered Questions

Everything finally boils down to a question mark.
No knowledge gained, no questions answered.
When you think you've grasped what you're looking for,
Something deeper throws you off, conflicting with what once
      was truth.
Life gives only a string of unanswered questions, great riddles
Which poets, theologians, and philosophers all try to solve.
Digging into the unknown is frustrating because there is no truth.
You accept what is most comfortable with your psyche
Like evolution, creationism, existentialism, absurdity.
Truth is a word with many meanings which themselves might
      not be true.
Life is absurd, sometimes damn pointless, some joys, some pains,
Some moments of lucidity, but mostly you are left in the dark,
Working life away too tired to wonder why or argue.
Those who question, destroy themselves with pain and confusion.
Every day I ask myself why I continue to question
But I know why: I was born like this.
I will banter, rave, and curse for the answer to life's validity.
I want to know; I write to know; I will die to know.

Disjointed Thoughts

Christ, I never thought it could happen:
My impenetrable wall is slowly crumbling.
My heart wants to believe in human kindness,
While my mind is waiting for the blade to sever the head.
My mind and heart wage war incessantly,
Never reaching that happy medium.
The caustic words uttered marking the trail of a fool,
The cold heart developed while making life barren and desolate,
The boredom developed when stuck in a routine
Can cause straightforward embarrassment
When life changes later and I'm left with an attitude.
To admit not knowing everything is hard to do.
To admit I'm not as strong as I think,
To admit I can't handle everything,
To admit I'm foolish and impetuous
Causes extreme joy and humility afterwards.
Embarrassment and regret are two fruitful feelings
Leading to a higher plane.
I know that no sense comes from extremism.
There is no total black and white,
So one doesn't have to shed integrity when change comes.
Accept the growth that comes from living with a free spirit.
Every year more and more security in my life disintegrates.
The chasm between the old and new becomes more distinguished.
The old bonds are loosening, and I don't know whether to cry
Or to be happy that someone has reached out to me.
Paranoia sets in when events seem too good to be true.
Complications arise when you trust someone with your mind.
I wish this peace could last forever, but it does not
And it will not sustain the spirit.

In Passing

Every day it is like life has been all too clarified.
All these years accumulating and racing by.
Childhood has passed, but it seems like yesterday.
Life does not wait for decisions,
Or the right time to accomplish something.
It leaves you as fast as it created you.
You expect to feel comfortable somewhere,
But life is not like that
Unless you want to define yourself somewhere.
Anxious, restless turnings in your mind.
As soon as the dust starts settling,
The wind picks up and spreads it everywhere again.
You can look back and feel all used up,
Like there is no umbilical cord
Connecting you to your past.
The present seems all too surreal,
The past a complete dream.
Trapped in a dream state,
Your future appears unclear.
Life and time are mere words.
Your mind controls your own passing of time.
You make it as you see fit.
Your actual existence is but a drop in a bucket
Compared to this universe and eternity.
It is what you do with time
That makes you perceive things the way you do,
And how you suppose time to be.

At some point in life you will hear
The ticking of the mortality clock,
And short picture clips of your life
Will play before your eyes, uncensored.
Then it will stop, and where will you be?
It is best to keep a constant projector
Running through your mind.
"Like sands through the hourglass,
So are the days of our lives."

To Be Able to Continue

The tears rolling down my face
Destroyed the mystique of my own self-imagined strength.
I was rigid.
Your gentle touch sent me into various levels of hell.
My disgusting weaknesses were all I could think about.
I did not feel self-absorbed,
All I craved was self-detachment,
Maybe a rendezvous with some exquisite form of danger.
My mind's eye sees too much blackness within other's hearts,
And only when it is blinded for a while am I at peace.
When you mentally break down into another's presence,
All you can want is complete solitude.
Nothing will remain the same
After all the walls have been destroyed.
Being constantly expected to become this,
Or become that causes me anguish.
Why do I have to be anything?
Why do I have to play the happy-go-lucky charade?
I am haunted by the notion of hidden ghosts within me.
Things I thought I had excreted long ago
Are so deeply rooted that I am a walking time bomb.
I feel fit in my mind, but does that make me sound?
I have understood the fact of creating one's own destiny,
But I'll be damned to know what mine is.
Change is inevitable,
But I'm stuck in my own warped thought pattern,
Refusing to accept upheaval.
I have no concept of changing emotions
Because I do not drift with the heartless tides.

Whether Real or Imagined

The tendency to overdramatize
Seems to be my problem.
Whether real or imagined
It does not matter,
The bullet in the mind
and the heart still is painful.
Brooding is part of my nature,
Life is too goddamn serious for me.
It is human nature
To want to read into simple things,
And to turn them into complex situations.
I cannot picture the total freedom of wings
Because all I know is the pounds of gravel
Which hold me down and anchor my soul
Into the cold concrete.
A smile of another flips into a scowl,
Laughter only seems mocking.
I take that charge I receive from another
And instantly have to gnaw on that feeling
Until I turn it negative.
I seem to run into or see into
Something that will only cause me harm.
Whether real or imagined does not matter,
The subjective pain is real enough.
There is no security
In this warped way of thought.

As much as it would be nice
To just let go
And laugh and not give a fuck,
I cannot.
That knife always appears in my mind
Slicing my peace of mind to shreds.
Is it other's flaws or mine,
Am I too on target,
Or missing it completely?
Self-introspection is never easy,
But by honesty and through catharsis
Others hardly seem as complex.
It is the level of high
Consciousness and memory
Which will cause an overt sensitivity
To ordinary situations.
It is the words which give an unexplainable feeling,
Some tangible word to tie into reality,
But sometimes words fail
Or lack complete enough structure.

Endurance

It is amazing how long people survive
Under horrible circumstances.
Our ability to exist
Comes from the human will,
The beauty of resolution
When the suffering is over.
I know others, and I feel shallow,
Pitiful and weak.
Triumphs come through endurance,
Endurance with a positive outlook.
It is the innate tendency for negativity
That fucks us up.
Through clenched, broken-down fists
And oceans of tears
Some can still see the light,
Exist and remember the good,
The times before the strife.
To survive, clarity has to be dimmed
Because some moments seem like eons.
One has to almost lie
To keep the soul from swallowing itself,
To keep suicide away.
The endurance to withstand that inner pain
Almost has to come from divine intervention.
It is a mystery.

Endurance is a positive means for survival.
I am too fucking vulnerable because of it,
But I will be damned if someone pities me.
If I lay in ruin, I did that to myself.
I cannot accept what cannot be changed,
So be it.
But I'm not asking for your understanding.
I don't expect understanding.
What I want is the freedom to complete this course
Which I feel will lead me somewhere.
I also want the strength to not be trampled
By my subjective demons.
Where the world might have driven me
Into this state, I let it.
I have myself to blame.

The Retired Man

Reflecting on life through closed eyes,
The old man sets down his coffee mug
And reclines in his chair.
The open window emits a slow breeze throughout the room.
The afternoon is unusually bright.
These are the moments when sleep is an uncontrollable narcotic
Which spreads throughout the body
Letting the man sink into a safe oblivion.
The eyes get completely murky and the lids shut upon themselves.
It is no longer painful to reflect
A history of pasts done and closed,
Shut away into the brain, action no longer necessary.
Life is winding down, days are spent by the window
Trying to figure out something less traumatic,
Less real, like the sun.
He needs nothing but this chair, the open window
And an empty mind in which to sink
Into the few moments of peace afforded
Now that life is almost over.

Very Little I Control

Life is powerless beyond the realm of the self.
This is the truth of the individual with expectations,
Realizing without a doubt that nothing can be
Absolutely expected of anyone.
Subjective desires exist in the head for a reason.
Dreams are easily dreamed or transferred
Into art forms, then left helpless
While reality shows them, as they are, only dreams.
People are not as easily transferred,
Nor do they accord to the subjective wills of others.
That is the first crash course in life
For all those unhappy daycare victims
Not yet realizing they are not gods.
Adults know this but still wish for the impossible.
Powerlessness is the dictator in all things
Eventually beyond the realm of self.

The Great Morning Tradition

It is something of a great morning tradition,
The coffee and the newspaper.
It is how many start their mornings,
Catching up on the news while awakening.
The mornings have always filled me with a vague, unsettling
     feeling,
Something that spreads from the stomach and fills the body.
I have never needed any help with fear,
And yet after briefly scanning the newspaper,
It is enough to make me rush back to bed and shut away the day.
To realize without any doubts that the news is ugly,
That people always hurt and that ignorance is pervasive,
Makes it hard to imagine how one could enjoy
Starting the day immersed in the pages of hell.

A Poem of Nothings

How badly I want to laugh or cry,
To have something within me feel alive, feel human
No matter how misconstrued that all is.
It is hard to see myself
Walking down an endless flight of stairs
Not knowing the outcome and only wishing for some resolve,
Good or bad, but at least something definite and real.
I eat these days up all in a row and know only hunger.
Everything tastes of stale air and the suffocating lack of oxygen
Affects the brain leaving it more resigned
And yet more desperate.
There is no substance here, there is no sense.
I keep up a steady conversation with myself;
Repeating empty words of solace,
But self-deceit only lasts so long.
Even these words are escaping me now
As I am hopelessly distracted on things which lack description.
It is 10:35 p.m., and I can't laugh, cry, or accept
So I just sit and wait and wait and wait

Irony, Innocence, and Honesty

My children talk about their day at school
While I sit listening and trying in vain
To forget about my yesterdays, today,
And all the days that follow of work.
My ironic life.
I was foolish enough to wish for this empty adulthood existence,
But even now I would not want my school years back.
Even with a great sense of humor,
Certain things you would not want to repeat.
Nothing worthwhile comes automatic,
Yet after fighting so hard for so little,
I feel chronically shortchanged.
Knowing this, being an ever-present witness and participant
In this waste, it is no wonder
That the days always end hinting of self-destruction.
Yet, it is on to tomorrow, and so on, and so on.
When my children finish with their reiterations of the day,
I am occasionally asked of mine,
And it is always hard to answer honestly.

Electrical Shortage

Just like the frayed cord in the hands of an electrician
The mind is to the heart.
Separate, although wanting the same,
The mind knows all about the pitfalls, the games,
The madness of functioning amongst others
Also caught in similar traps.
The heart knows no peace,
Struggling every day with what the mind knows.
The courage of the heart quelled daily to compliance,
But suffering because the mind can neither fathom nor find
The key to the heart's needs.
Knowledge can kill more than create.
Realizing does not mean solutions,
Life does not mean fairness,
And the human body is not fortified
To the point of immunity from itself and others.

Blaring Sirens

Staring at the tranquil afternoon sky with heavy-lidded eyes,
The fingers hold the cigarette, the blue-gray smoke
Moves with slow thickness towards the ceiling.
Time stands still.
The feeling is one of sick oppression
As dizziness sets in
Along with the now more frequent pains.
Health has been slipping for some time,
Youth long gone.
The cigarette drops almost imperceptibly,
The mouth agape, stricken with sudden intense pain.
The sky no longer looks tranquil
As those tired well-worn lidded eyes glass over,
Staring at this soon approaching eternity of gray.
Aware of now being one with the floor,
The voice in the other room calling you,
Calling you, calling 911,
The sirens now sound off in the distance.
Memories come flooding too quick for understanding,
Just futile attempts at trying to redeem this life.
The sirens now become louder and louder.
The focus wavers, now comes the waves of rest.
The sirens pass by and as I move away
I ponder your fate wondering
What mine will be.

Narcotic-Paced Minutes

It happens quite often,
The sickness of immobility
When it seems everything has drained away from your essence
And is impossible to move.
Time moves forward at a narcotic pace.
The mind draws blanks over and over,
And the eyes stare straight ahead,
But you focus on nothing.
You hear voices, but they register as jumbled noise.
It is far from a daydream
Because it is a blankness that overwhelms.
It is a stupor created from disgust, from boredom,
From knowing that you will have to endure
Countless minutes that always bring with them a feeling of
    living death.

They Hate the Living Artists But Love the Dead Ones

After a while they will tell you to shut up,
To quit your screaming, to act right
As if you are a complete fool or somewhat deranged.
It is as if they have grown tired of the repetition,
The same old horror escaping from your lips
Which they never understood and could not quite see.
The problem here is that everyone wants happiness,
But what they ignore or choose to swallow
You cannot, and it makes them angry.
People can appreciate certain concepts from a distance,
Or at least they claim to appreciate,
Yet when anything unsettling hits close to home,
Then all of a sudden the appreciation is gone.
Anytime one tries to escape the bounds of the mediocre mind,
It is never favorably noticed.
Hell is what you catch,
Hell is what you find,
And time and time again
You will be ostracized, silenced, told to shut up,
To quit your silliness.
You will only find a loneliness
Which is proof enough of a certain truth.

More Than Just a Weekend Escape

It is always nice because it happens so rarely,
The chance to escape for a day or so,
To become anonymous in foreign surroundings.
The feeling of a strange hotel room
Gives me a sense of peace, a feeling of freedom.
This brief respite is an affirmation of life,
And it is easily realized how little we live
Most of the time.
If only there could be an eternity
To lie in this bed and lazily sip beer,
To play cards with my wife
While watching the sky's colors
Become engulfed with darkness,
To enjoy passionate, unhurried love,
To have everything exist in this short time
Free of work or difficulty,
To fully live each minute
Instead of just being aware of the passing of time,
To shut out the world and regroup what is left.

There Is No Real Humanity

People do not let each other live.
They refuse the concept of harmony.
They would rather gnash their teeth
And strike out until they feel someone's defeat is inevitable.
There is nothing I have seen
To contradict the horrible nature of the human soul.
There is no satisfying or quelling the viciousness in humanity.
It is a mockery of life.
I cannot enjoy what others claim to.
I am not them.
I do not expect to ever feel content
Living in the boundaries of being human.
Conflicts are a constant reality.
When the mind and heart become so fucked up and junked,
Life is lived through tunnel vision and nothing is enjoyed.

What to Do While Waiting for the Final Curtain

To be fully aware of what taking a breath means,
To be fully aware of how bizarre and unfathomable thought is,
Becomes a responsibility almost too painful to endure
Once lucid of actually living.
We live, but without really knowing how electrical that is.
How tragic is the realization of wasted years
In a world where people are threatened with time.
Until the taste of death fills my mouth
And closes my thoughts will I know
Just how well I fulfilled my obligation to myself.
Thoughts are meaningless until truly tested.
If they hold up, then something was won in this life,
Which only gives that responsibility
And no help with answers.

Something Eventually Gives Out

It seems like such a mockery of life,
This lack of understanding between people.
I know a one-sided form of communication with paper.
There is nothing promised between people,
No golden umbilical cord to unite.
Ideas frightfully exist alone.
It takes tremendous courage
To withstand the contempt misunderstanding brings.
There are times when it feels as if my head will explode,
So detached am I from my surroundings.
Everything within my grasp seems light years away,
And yet I have to contend with the reality of a modern man
Who is never allowed the blessed recesses children have.
What will become of future years is beyond me,
Since dealing with tomorrow is already too much.
I live on a permanent leash just like everyone else,
Yet know I cannot accept surrendering like a dog,
But this knowledge is futile.
People, just like animals when sick and no longer of use,
Become disposed of one way or another.
It is only a matter of time before I tire of myself
Or become retired by society.
Where is the victory in those choices?

9 7 9 8 8 9 0 6 1 3 2 0 2